america

Standard Book Number: 0-914308-00-9

Published by KARO COMMUNICATIONS, INC., Los Angeles, California 91401.

Printed in the United States of America.

First Edition.

Photographed by Ron Rubenstein
Photographs 9 and 12 by James Bell
(in order of appearance)

dedication

To those who know their own weakness well enough
To understand America's mistakes
To heal her wounds
To struggle for change.
To those who care enough about America
To see the beauty beyond arrogance
To remember a young land with noble goals
But especially to those
Who dare to dream dreams without certainty of success.

AMERICA

A Ballad by
JAMES KAVANAUGH

Art Direction/Design
by Ron Rubenstein

KARO COMMUNICATIONS, INC.
Los Angeles, California

introduction

It never occurred to me to write a poem about America. It just seemed to happen, as poems sometimes do, and feelings poured forth which surprised me.

I love America, deeply and personally. Often she has disappointed me but so have my closest friends. Often she has caused me pain but so has everyone I've ever loved.

I am not a naive citizen. I have spent time in many other lands, lived there, studied there, taught there. I have travelled this entire land, known well several of her greatest cities, ridden her rivers, camped in her forests, swam in her oceans, wandered her deserts, laughed and drank in her village bars. I was raised in a small town, moved to a metropolis, returned to a village, then to the giant city again. I know the south from the north and New York from California.

I have challenged America in writings and in lectures, I have criticized her in essays and conversations. But I spoke and wrote as a son, who would rather live here than anywhere else in the world. Not because this is the greatest land in the world, not because it is the most powerful or the most human, not because it is the most noble or the most free—simply because it is my land and I love her.

I love the openness and simplicity of her people, their courage and humility, their warmth and humanness. I know we have sometimes neglected the poor but we have also tried honestly to help them. I know we have oppressed the minorities but finally we have begun to do something about it. I know we have fought pointless wars, but it was the protest of our own people that changed our course.

Some of us came here willingly from Europe and Asia and the rest of the world. Some of us came to find freedom, some simply to find food and hope. Some were dragged here against their will. But most of us are still here, determined to make of this land what we know it can be. For the most part, we have been a land of individuals and malcontents in our origins, and this, if anything, has given us a special energy.

We have weathered revolutions before, we have known crisis, endured war and depression, faced unspeakable tragedies. Our leaders have been assassinated, our youth murdered, our dreams destroyed. But we have always come back—more determined and wiser. We are a young country grown suddenly old, a light-hearted land grown suddenly solemn, a brave land grown deeply afraid.

But we have begun to re-evaluate our institutions, to assess our values, to sort out our priorities. We have challenged our leaders in high places, confronted our churches, our universities, our business conglomerates. Most of all, we have begun to look into our own hearts.

This is a ballad about America, written by an American. It comes simply from his heart. And he still believes what he learned as a small boy: that if we truly become "a nation of the people, by the people, for the people", no matter what, "we shall not perish from the earth!"

You've grown old, my country,
And I never even noticed.
Suddenly one day your hair turned grey,
There was a tired look in your eyes.
You knew your children were too big now
To shout into silence.
Once you stroked their hair,
Told them tales of brave men.
Now there is sullenness and weariness,
You are not strong enough to raise your hand.

I love you, America,
But not like I used to
When you were a fable without weakness.
You sent your sons to war,
Your children to school,
You sent your men to work,
Your women to tend the home.
There was grumbling.
But there was obedience.
It seemed a nice land then,
Some may not remember.
We studied soldiers' medals,
Whispered when we saw a purple heart.
Mothers kept stars in their windows
And boys who gave their lives
Really died for their country.

But you've grown old, America,
Minute men are a dusty memory,
George Washington as distant as a textbook.
I know that Lincoln learned his law by lamp,
But meanwhile John was killed, and Robert,
Malcolm fell and Martin.

RICA

AME

I don't know what happened,
But suddenly the war was at home.
Maybe it was always that way
    In secret corners
       In wounds inflicted unwittingly
         In sadness no one would understand
        In silence.

I know you wanted peace, America,
But there was no peace,
And it was your own fault!
You talked of freedom,
Of equality and justice,
You taught us to yearn and ask,
To fight and grow,
You told us stories of little men made big,
Told us tales of success
And success was always monuments and money.

We wanted other things, America,
We thought you understood,
Time for love and laughing,
Freedom from slavery—and dignity,
Music on the streets—and flowers.
Sometimes we didn't know what we wanted.
But it had to be more than we had!

You have grown so serious, America,
So dull and deathlike,
So solemn and frightened!
Now we do not kill ducks and deer,
We kill each other.
We save the Siberian tiger
And destroy ourselves.

We are not one land, but many, America,
And our certainties and absolutes grow diffident.
Can we hear the black and brown man long enough
To comprehend his hostility and hurt?
Can we hear the white man
Who has only known slavery of another kind?
Can we hear the screams of women,
The shouts and cynicism of the young,
The cries and fears of the old?

I am tired, too, America,
Tired of the disloyal spouting their loyalties,
Of the greedy preaching forebearance,
Of despots demanding discipline and docility,
Tired of men and women calling angry theories God,
Of the oppressed becoming the oppressor,
Of hostile eyes and hate filled words,
Tired of persons looking everywhere but within themselves!

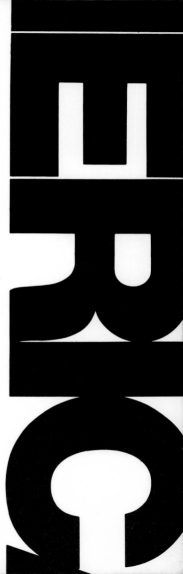

merica

Your childhood is over, America,
And your adolescence.
Noisy protests seem like high school pep rallies.
Some of us want life now!
Our pain is too deep for slogans,
Our anger too profound for placards,
Our hurt too raw for discussion!

How do you tell your father he is narrow and unforgiving?
How do you tell your mother she is unfeeling and biased?
Maybe in the beginning, nations, like frightened men,
Must shout their power,
Flex their muscles, feign infallible.
But when an old man is arrogant,
Somehow you know it's too late!
When an old man blusters and brags,
Somehow you know he's never been well loved!

Grow soft, America, and let the wrinkles show!
Grow gentle, America, let the mistakes be revealed!
Grow wise, America, let your scars be seen.
Men will scorn a flag that scorns them,
Leave a land that leaves them.
But they will love a land that loves them,
And trust a land that is as weak as they are!

There is no salvation on the battlefields, America,
War creates bitterness and brutal memories,
And the treaty of peace is only preamble to another war.

There is no salvation in the churches, America,
God became as grey and cultish as those who made him.

There is no salvation in economics, America,
Only the juggling of figures to seduce men
And make them believe they can possess what cannot be bought.

There is only salvation in the hearts of men and women
Who are not tied to their possessions
Or bound to their successes,
Who are not chained to their ego
Or buried in past bitterness,
Those who can reach out and give!

Some cannot give,
So much has been taken from them!
Some cannot understand,
For they have never been heard!
Some cannot love,
For they have never been well loved!
But some of us know the beginning of love,
Who can nourish the empty and distressed,
Who can give to those who have nothing to give.

Perhaps we cannot give much,
Or give long.
But we can give!
Not for God! Or country! Or nobility!
Simply for our brothers!
For no reason at all.